OUT OF THE LAB
EXTREME JOBS IN SCIENCE

CLIMATOLOGISTS AND METEOROLOGISTS

by Ruth Owen

PowerKiDS press

New York

Published in 2014 by The Rosen Publishing Group, Inc.
29 East 21st Street, New York, NY 10010

First Edition

Produced for Rosen by Ruby Tuesday Books Ltd
Editor for Ruby Tuesday Books Ltd: Mark J. Sachner
US Editor: Joshua Shadowens
Designer: Tammy West and Emma Randall

Photo Credits:
Cover, 17 © Superstock; cover, 7 (bottom), 8–9, 13, 14–15, 20–21, 23 © Shutterstock; 4–5, 18–19 © Science Photo Library; 7 (top), 29 © NASA; 10–11 © Wikipedia Creative Commons; 23 (center) © Public Domain; 23 (bottom) © istockphoto; 1, 24–25 © NOAA; 27 © U.S. Air Force 403rd Wing.

Publisher Cataloging Data

Owen, Ruth.
Climatologists and meteorologists / by Ruth Owen. — First edition.
   p. cm. — (Out of the lab: extreme jobs in science)
Includes index.
ISBN 978-1-4777-1288-7 (library binding) — ISBN 978-1-4777-1376-1 (pbk.) — ISBN 978-1-4777-1377-8 (6-pack)
1. Climatology — Vocational guidance — Juvenile literature. 2. Meteorology — Vocational guidance — Juvenile literature. 3. Climatologists — Juvenile literature. 4. Meteorologists — Juvenile literature. I. Owen, Ruth, 1967–. II. Title.
QC863.5 O94 2014
551.6'023—dc23

Manufactured in the United States of America

CPSIA Compliance Information: Batch #S13PK8: For Further Information contact Rosen Publishing, New York, New York at 1-800-237-9932

Contents

DRILLING FOR ANSWERS

Out on the blinding white Antarctic ice, in temperatures of just −9°F (−23°C), a team of scientists is gathering ice core samples.

The scientists are using a tube-shaped drill that cuts into the ice and removes a long section, or core. Over several weeks, the team has drilled deep into the ice and now have an ice core sample that's 2,100 feet (650 m) long. The ice in the very deepest parts of the core is tens of thousands of years old.

The group of scientists are **climatologists** and they have braved many weeks working and living in extreme conditions to find out what this ancient ice can tell us about our **climate** and **climate change**.

SCIENCE IN ACTION

An ice core drill works in the same way as an apple corer that removes the center from a piece of fruit. The ice core samples are drilled from the ice in sections that each measure 3 feet (1 m) long.

Scientists collecting ice core samples in Antarctica ▼

Ice core sample

Ice core drill

WHAT IS A CLIMATOLOGIST?

Climatologists are scientists who study climate. Climate and **weather** often get mixed up, but they are not the same thing.

Weather is what happens in an area over a few days or weeks. Climate, however, is what happens in an area over 30 years or more. Using temperature and **precipitation** records, climatologists work out average temperatures and average amounts of rainfall or snowfall to calculate what an area's normal weather is like. They then use these long-term records to **forecast** how an area's climate might change in the future.

One of the big issues we face today is climate change, so many climatologists are studying how Earth's climate is changing and what it could mean for life on Earth.

SCIENCE IN ACTION

Climatologists may spend some time out of the lab carrying out **fieldwork**. They also work in **laboratories** and spend a lot of time working on computers creating **computer models** that use historic data to predict what an area's climate might be like in the future.

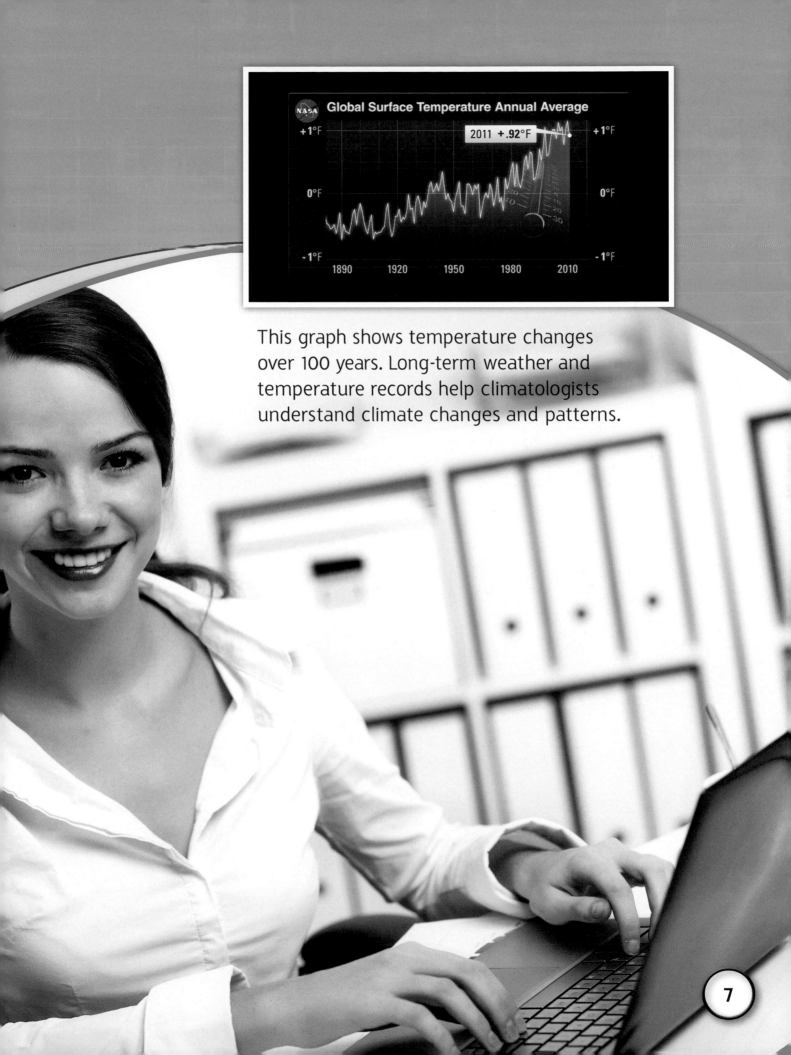

Global Surface Temperature Annual Average

2011 +.92°F

This graph shows temperature changes over 100 years. Long-term weather and temperature records help climatologists understand climate changes and patterns.

WHAT IS CLIMATE CHANGE?

Climate change is a gradual change in Earth's temperatures. At this moment in time, our planet is warming up.

Changes in temperature can happen naturally. Most scientists agree, however, that the current increase in Earth's temperatures is being caused by human activities.

When we burn oil in vehicles or coal in a power plant to make electricity, gases such as carbon dioxide are released into the Earth's **atmosphere**. These gases are known as **greenhouse gases**. This is because they trap the Sun's heat on Earth in the way that a greenhouse traps heat inside. We need heat and light to survive, but too much heat will cause big problems. Warmer temperatures will cause ocean levels to rise because water expands when it is heated. This could cause flooding in many parts of the world.

SCIENCE IN ACTION

While some parts of the world flood, climate change will make others so hot and dry that people will have trouble growing food. Lakes and rivers will also dry up, making it hard for people and animals to find enough water.

Warmer temperatures will mean some places will struggle to grow crops for food.

Burning gas in cars and burning coal to make electricity create gases that are causing climate change.

ANCIENT CLIMATES

How do we know that burning fuel and creating greenhouse gases is causing climate change?

We wouldn't know if it wasn't for the work of scientists, such as climatologists, who research these issues and look for evidence.

Examining Antarctic ice core samples is one way that climatologists have been able to compare Earth's past climate to today's climate. The ice cores are like timelines stretching back thousands of years. Trapped inside the ice are small bubbles of air from different times in Earth's history. Scientists have analyzed this air to find out how much carbon dioxide and other gases it contains. The answer came back that the amount of greenhouse gases in the air has risen dramatically in the past 100 years.

SCIENCE IN ACTION

The longest ice core ever collected was 2.2 miles (3.7 km) long. It contained information about Earth's climate that stretched back 800,000 years!

Ice core samples are stored at Antarctic temperatures in large freezers at laboratories and other research centers around the world.

The ice in this ice core sample is 16,250 years old. Each of the lines represents a year.

EXTREME SCIENCE, EXTREME LIVES

When climatologists and other scientists are doing research in Antarctica, they may spend weeks or months camping in tents.

Pyramid-shaped tents are used because they withstand the fierce winds. Sometimes a whiteout occurs. This is when very low clouds seem to blend in with the white, snowy ground making it impossible to see more than a few feet (m) ahead. On these days, scientists work in their tents and do not go out.

When camping on a field trip in Antarctica, meals include **freeze-dried** meals that are mixed with water, dried soup, dried vegetables, cookies, chocolate, oatmeal, and drinks such as tea, coffee, and hot chocolate. Water is made by melting snow over small camping stoves.

SCIENCE IN ACTION

Climatologists often work in teams with scientists from other parts of the world. This can make good sense because issues such as climate change affect every country and every person on the planet.

This small tent pitched on the Antarctic ice may be a scientist's home for a few months!

MIXING SCIENCE WITH ADVENTURE

Climatologist Kim Cobb describes herself as being about 20 percent Indiana Jones. That's because this scientist not only studies Earth's climate, but scuba dives, climbs, and spends time in deep caves.

Kim's fieldwork takes her out of the lab to gather evidence of what our climate was like in the past. One way that Kim collects data is by gathering samples of **corals**. She collects some samples by scuba diving on coral reefs in tropical oceans. She also collects coral **fossils** from beaches. When she analyzes the chemicals in these long-lived sea creatures, the chemical data gives her information about Earth's past climate. Kim can find out what temperatures and even rainfall were like for the past 50 to 1,000 years.

SCIENCE IN ACTION

In order to predict future climate patterns, scientists must know what patterns have happened in the past. People have only kept climate records for about 150 years. In nature, however, there are chemical records stored in corals, ice, tree rings, **sediments**, and many other natural materials.

Scientists wearing scuba diving gear carry out research on a coral reef.

Fossil corals

COLLECTING STALAGMITE SAMPLES

Kim Cobb doesn't only gather samples on the seabed. She also leads cave expeditions to collect samples of stalagmites.

In the Gunung Mulu National Park on the island of Borneo, in Asia, Kim and her team climb into large caves. There, they collect pieces of fallen or broken stalagmites and drill for samples in growing stalagmites.

Just like corals, the chemicals inside stalagmite samples give Kim valuable information about the historical climate in the area. When fed into computer models, this data can tell Kim what should have happened naturally to Earth's climate at this moment in time and what has happened because of human activities.

SCIENCE IN ACTION

A stalagmite is a column made from minerals, such as calcium carbonate, which is a substance found in rocks, seashells, and eggshells. Water containing minerals drips from a cave's ceiling, and over time, the minerals build up on the cave floor growing into a stalagmite. Columns that grow down from a cave's ceiling are called stalactites.

Stalagmites and stalactites inside a cave at Gunung Mulu National Park, Borneo

WHAT IS A METEOROLOGIST?

Meteorology is the scientific study of Earth's atmosphere and the events that take place in the atmosphere. These include rain, snow, cloud cover, wind, temperature, lightning, and other conditions that make up the weather across our planet.

Meteorologists are scientists who study the atmosphere. They may work for government agencies that are concerned with weather and conditions in the atmosphere. These include **NASA** and the National Weather Service, which studies weather patterns, makes forecasts, and issues warnings for tornadoes, severe thunderstorms, and other dangerous weather.

Meteorologists also perform research at universities and public utilities, such as water and electric companies. They are best known as radio and television weather forecasters.

Researchers studying a supercell thunderstorm, which is a severe storm that can produce a tornado.

In order to research extreme weather such as **tornadoes** and supercell thunderstorms, some meteorologists may go out into the field to chase these extreme weather phenomena. These scientists place themselves directly in the path of a storm in vehicles fitted with instruments that take measurements and collect data.

OUT OF THE STUDIO AND INTO THE WEATHER

Today, TV meteorologists are taking their weather forecasts out of the studio and into the elements.

Most of the work that television meteorologists do takes place inside the studio. There, meteorologists analyze the information provided by their instruments and prepare their on-air weather forecasts. Many TV stations, however, have areas, sometimes called "weather decks," where meteorologists take their weather reports outdoors, often in the middle of raging blizzards, thunderstorms, and hurricanes. There, viewers can watch weather happening in "real time."

Of course, the conditions that are most interesting are usually not the most comfortable, or even the safest. But this kind of reporting has turned TV weather into something that viewers can relate to!

A TV meteorologist makes his weather ➤ report standing in rising floodwaters.

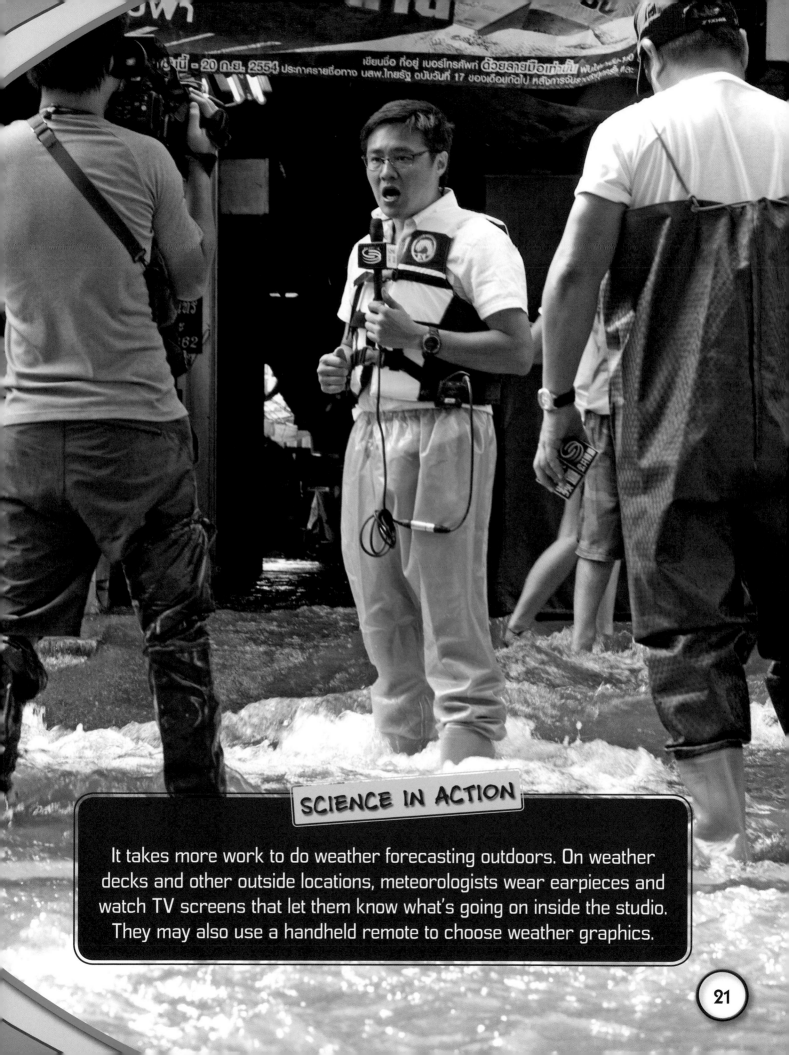

SCIENCE IN ACTION

It takes more work to do weather forecasting outdoors. On weather decks and other outside locations, meteorologists wear earpieces and watch TV screens that let them know what's going on inside the studio. They may also use a handheld remote to choose weather graphics.

THE MORE EXTREME, THE BETTER!

Television viewers expect weather broadcasts that not only report the weather but bring it into their homes live and up-close.

This is especially true during severe weather. For example, in 2012, national weather people reported in conditions so extreme that they were often swept off their feet by wind, rain, and raging floodwaters.

At local TV stations as well, many meteorologists gave eyewitness accounts of "Superstorm Sandy" from the same streets and waterfronts that endangered the lives of ordinary citizens. All of this was part of a job that meteorologists do every day, but not in such extreme conditions. That job is not just to forecast the weather, but to educate viewers and to dramatize the dangers of severe weather.

A TV weather reporter talks to the camera under extreme conditions!

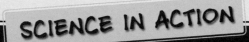

SCIENCE IN ACTION

National Weather Service meteorologists are responsible for the severe-weather warnings that often interrupt TV and radio broadcasts. These warnings give exact places and times for the danger and instruct people to take shelter until the emergency is over.

```
EMERGENCY ALERT SYSTEM
ng counties: McHenry IL.  E

National Weather Service

Issued a

Tornado Warning
```

A National Weather Service warning

THE EYE OF THE STORM

A meteorologist is looking from the window of a plane. Beyond the glass, he sees that the aircraft is surrounded by a bowl-shaped wall of white clouds.

The scientist is onboard the plane to study weather. This is no ordinary weather, however. The plane is in the eye, or center, of a massive hurricane!

Scientist Jack Parrish is a meteorologist and a hurricane hunter. In his career, he has flown into the eye of a hurricane hundreds of times. Along with the plane's crew and other scientists onboard, the team of hurricane hunters has flown into one of the most dangerous and extreme types of weather on Earth in order to study it!

SCIENCE IN ACTION

A hurricane is a large, powerful storm that begins life over an ocean. A hurricane may be 600 miles (966 km) wide. Its swirling circle of winds can reach speeds of 200 miles per hour (322 km/h).

This WP-3D Orion and Gulfstream IV aircraft are hurricane-hunting planes operated by the NOAA (National Oceanic and Atmospheric Administration).

This image was taken by hurricane hunters inside the eye of Hurricane Katrina.

EXTREME DATA COLLECTION

Hurricane hunters fly low into the bottom of a hurricane. Sometimes they are flying at just 1,000 feet (300 m) above the ground.

It might seem like the eye of the hurricane would be the storm's most dangerous area, but actually, once inside the swirling clouds, conditions in the eye are quite calm. From inside the hurricane, the scientists drop a piece of equipment called a dropsonde from the plane. A dropsonde is described as a tube fitted with scientific instruments and a parachute!

The dropsonde descends through the hurricane into the ocean below. On its journey down, it transmits information back to the plane that hurricane forecasters can use to decide if the storm is getting weaker or growing stronger.

SCIENCE IN ACTION

The NOAA hurricane hunters don't just fly missions in the United States. They travel around the world, flying over oceans, mountains, wetlands, and even the Arctic. They gather data on many different types of weather.

A hurricane hunter prepares a dropsonde as his plane flies into a hurricane.

A SCIENCE CAREER WITH ADVENTURE

Most climate or weather scientists spend their days in offices or laboratories. Some, however, use their scientific training to do research in Earth's most extreme places or study our planet's most dangerous weather phenomena.

Will people be able to grow crops or have enough water in the future? The answers to these questions are important and will come from the work of climatologists. As a meteorologist, providing accurate weather forecasts is important work, too. Sometimes, it can even save lives!

Would you fly into a hurricane or crawl into a dark cave to collect samples? If you want to combine science with adventure, perhaps becoming a meteorologist or climatologist is the career for you!

SCIENCE IN ACTION

Meteorology has nothing to do with **meteors**, despite its name. The word "meteorology" comes from the Greek word *meteoros*, which means "high up" or "above." For the ancient Greeks, "meteorology" meant the study of anything that occurred in the atmosphere, from weather to meteors!

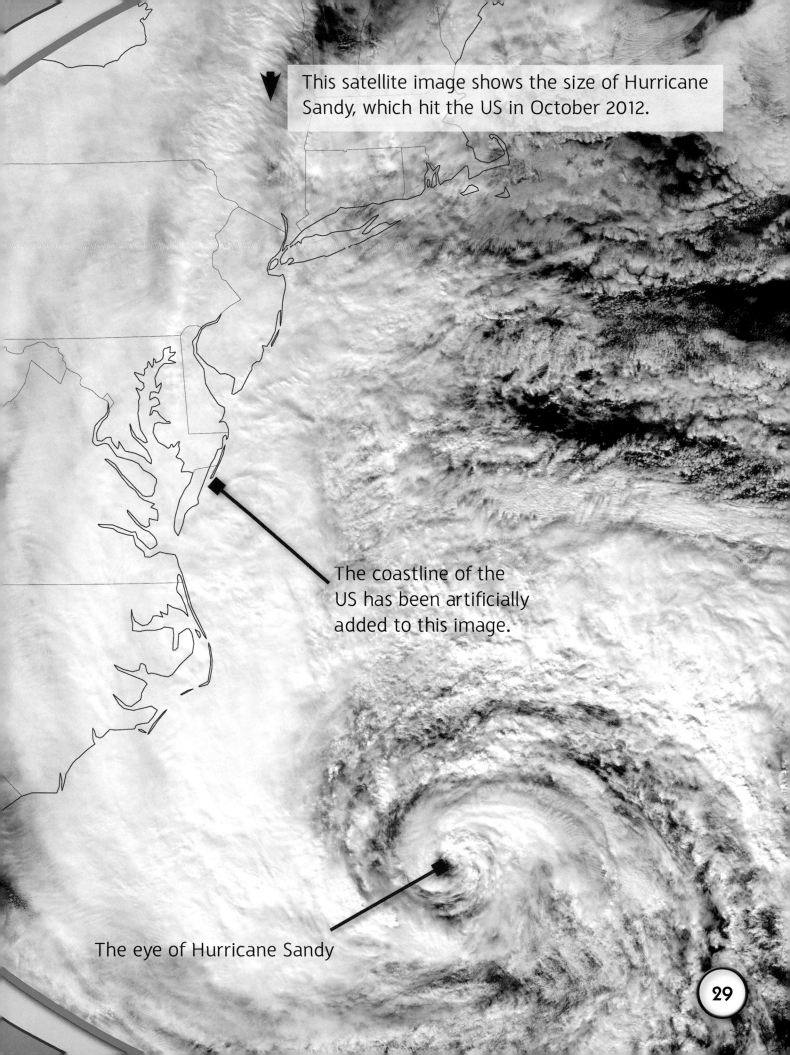

This satellite image shows the size of Hurricane Sandy, which hit the US in October 2012.

The coastline of the US has been artificially added to this image.

The eye of Hurricane Sandy

GLOSSARY

atmosphere (AT-muh-sfeer) The layer of gases surrounding a planet, moon, or star.

climate (KLY-mut) The average weather conditions in an area over a period of 30 years or more.

climate change (KLY-mut CHAYNJ) The gradual change in temperatures on Earth. For example, the current warming of temperatures caused by a buildup of greenhouse gases in the atmosphere.

climatologists (kly-muh-TO-luh-jists) Scientists who study Earth's climate.

computer models (kum-PYOO-ter MAH-dulz) Simulations or virtual situations that are created on a computer using data. A computer model can be manipulated to predict how a sequence of events might happen in the future.

corals (KOR-ulz) Tiny ocean animals that are joined together. When corals die, their rocklike skeletons remain to form a hard mass of matter known as a coral reef.

fieldwork (FEELD-wurk) Scientific work that takes place outside instead of in a laboratory.

forecast (FOR-kast) A prediction of something that will happen in the future, particularly in relation to weather.

fossil (FO-sul) An imprint of an animal's or plant's remains that has formed in rock over millions of years.

freeze-dried (FREEZ-dryd) Preserved by freezing and then drying so that all the moisture is removed.

greenhouse gases (GREEN-hows GAS-ez) Gases such as carbon dioxide, methane, and nitrous oxide that occur naturally and are also released into Earth's atmosphere when fossils fuels, such as coal and oil, are burned.

laboratories
(LA-buh-ruh-tawr-eez)
Rooms, buildings, and sometimes vehicles where there is equipment that can be used to carry out experiments and other scientific studies.

meteorology
(mee-tee-uh-RAH-luh-jee)
The scientific study of Earth's atmosphere and the events, such as weather, that take place there.

meteors (MEE-tee-orz) The streaks of light made by pieces of rock or dust as they burn up in Earth's atmosphere.

NASA (NAS-ah) The National Aeronautics and Space Administration, an organization in the United States that studies space and builds spacecraft.

precipitation
(pri-sip-ih-TAY-shun)
The different forms that water takes when it falls from clouds, for example, rain and snow.

sediment (SEH-deh-ment)
Tiny pieces of rock that have been worn away from bigger rocks by forces such as waves or wind.

tornadoes (tawr-NAY-dohz)
Violent, whirling columns of air that begin life in a thunderstorm cloud then drop down to the ground and move fast over land causing destruction.

weather (WEH-thur)
How hot or cold it is and other conditions such as rain, snow, wind, and hurricanes.

WEBSITES

Due to the changing nature of Internet links, PowerKids Press has developed an online list of websites related to the subject of this book. This site is updated regularly. Please use this link to access the list:

www.powerkidslinks.com/olejs/clim/

READ MORE

Bassett, John. *Experiments with Weather and Climate*. Cool Science. New York: Gareth Stevens Learning Library, 2010.

Housel, Debra J., and Robin S. Doak. *Investigating Storms*. Mission: Science. Mankato, MN: Compass Point Books, 2010.

Peterson, Judy Monroe. *Weather Watchers: Climate Scientists*. Extreme Scientists. New York: PowerKids Press, 2008.

INDEX